FLOW[ER]S
FOR FLOSSie

by Chenille Davis
illustrated by John Hovell

HOUGHTON MIFFLIN   BOSTON

Printed in China

ISBN 10: 0-618-88640-0
ISBN 13: 978-0-618-88640-1

6789 0940 16 15 14 13
4500411350

Skip wants flowers.
He wants them for Flossie.

How many flowers does Skip have?

Skip wants 9 flowers.
This one smells sweet.

How many flowers does Skip have?

Skip looks for more.
He sees 3 flowers.

How many flowers does Skip have all together?

Skip likes red.
He finds 2 red flowers.

How many flowers will Skip have now?

Hooray! Here are 3 more.
Skip picks 3 white flowers.

How many flowers does Skip have in all?

Skip has 9 flowers.
Flowers for Flossie!

Responding

Math Concepts

Make a Bouquet

Draw Visualize
Draw a picture of a flower Skip picked.

Tell About
1. Look at page 5.
2. Tell someone how many red flowers Skip found.

Write
Write how many flowers Skip has for Flossie.